W9-BWQ-574

IF YOU WERE RAISED BY A DINOSAUR

Isabella Brooklyn

Illustrated by Haude Levesque

imagine!
Publishing

New York
www.imaginebks.com

Text copyright © 2010 by Sudipta Bardham Quallen
Illustrations copyright © 2010 by Imagine Publishing, Inc.

Published by Imagine Publishing, Inc., 25 Whitman Road, Morganville, NJ 07751

Distributed in the United States of America by
BookMasters Distribution Services, Inc., 30 Amberwood Parkway, Ashland, OH 44805

Distributed in Canada by
BookMasters Distribution Services, Inc., c/o Jacqueline Gross Associates, 165 Dufferin Street,
Toronto, Ontario, Canada M6K 3H6

Distributed in the United Kingdom by
Publishers Group UK, 8 The Arena, Mollison Avenue, Enfield, EN3 7NL, UK

Library of Congress Cataloging-in-Publication Data
Brooklyn, Isabella.
If you were raised by a dinosaur / Isabella Brooklyn ; illustrated by Haude Levesque.
p. cm.
ISBN 978-1-936140-17-6 (hardcover : alk. paper)
1. Dinosaurs—Juvenile literature. 2. Dinosaurs—Behavior—Juvenile literature.
3. Dinosaurs—Growth—Juvenile literature. 4. Parental behavior
in animals—Juvenile literature.
I. Levesque, Haude, ill. II. Title.
QE861.5.B757 2010
567.9—dc22
2010001393

Designed by Marc Cheshire
Printed in China
Manufactured in April 2010

Contents

If You Were Raised By a Dinosaur

PEOPLE DO IT EVERY DAY. So do birds, monkeys, butterflies, and platypuses. We have babies.

For the 160 million years that the dinosaurs walked the earth, they did it, too.

Every living animal reproduces in some way, but how each cares for its young differs from species to species. Humans buy them toys, create nurseries, and organize playdates. Birds built nests and sit patiently on their eggs to warm them with their own body heat. After the eggs hatch, the parents provide food and protection until the chicks are ready to take care of themselves. Sea turtles also build nests for their eggs. But once the eggs have been laid, the mother leaves them behind and never returns. The father sea turtle isn't involved at all.

It's hard for **paleontologists** to know for sure how dinosaurs took care of their babies. After all, there are no living dinosaurs

All living animals reproduce, but how they care for their young differs from species to species.

to observe in their natural environments. The only way scientists have to learn about dinosaurs and their parenting techniques is by studying the clues that have been left behind. But even this is easier said than done.

The first dinosaurs appeared 230 million years ago, and the last to walk the earth were around until about 65 million years ago. That's a really long time for fossils to wait to be **excavated**! Scientists have found lots of adult dinosaur bones, but the bones of young dinosaurs are harder to find. Their smaller, less-formed skeletons are easily damaged by trampling feet, geological shifts, or the jaws (and digestive systems) of hungry **predators**.

Still, there are many things we have come to know—or at least think we know—about dinosaur mommies, daddies, and babies. But to understand all of this, we need to start at the beginning.

WHO WERE THE DINOSAURS?

The geological timescale is divided into three eras: the Paleozoic, the Mesozoic, and the Cenozoic. The Paleozoic era lasted from 250 to 550 million years ago. During this era, amphibians, fish, and land plants ruled the earth. Next came the Mesozoic era. The Mesozoic era is divided into the Triassic, Jurassic, and Cretaceous periods. The first dinosaurs evolved during the Triassic period, between 206 and 250 million years ago. During the Jurassic period, which extended from 144 to 204 million years ago, the number of

Scientists learn about dinosaurs
by studying their bones.

dinosaur species expanded, and the first birds appeared. Flowering plants came into being and dinosaurs became extinct in the Cretaceous period. The Cenozoic era, which is the period we live in, started 65 million years ago. Mammals, including humans, evolved during this time.

One of the problems that scientists face when studying fossils is that not all bones from millions of years ago are actually from dinosaurs. In addition to birds and plants, dinosaurs shared the earth with other reptiles, like aquatic plesiosaurs, flying pterosaurs, and land-dwelling *Dimetrodons*. They even walked alongside some ancient mammals, like the badger-sized *Didelphodon*—which likely scavenged dinosaur eggs for food—and *Repenomamus robustus*, whose fossil was found with the remains of a small dinosaur in its stomach. These creatures are often grouped with dinosaurs, but they definitely were not.

When scientists talk about dinosaurs (a term coined by Sir Richard Owen in 1842 that means "terrifying lizard"), they mean a specific group of reptiles that lived only in the Mesozoic era. Paleontologists look at several factors to decide if the fossil they have found comes from a dinosaur.

First, dinosaurs lived only on land. There is no evidence that any dinosaur could fly, and though many species lived near bodies of water, they definitely did not live in the water.

Dinosaurs shared the earth with lots of other animals.

Second, dinosaurs had an upright posture. That means they walked with their legs directly under their torsos. This feature was important to the way dinosaurs evolved in size. When an animal has legs that sprawl out from under its body like an alligator, it is difficult to grow very large. Legs that come out at an angle like that make it hard to support a lot of weight and still remain mobile. On the other hand, when an animal's legs are underneath its body, like humans, they can support a lot of weight and the animal can grow very, very large and still be able to get around. In fact, dinosaurs were the first vertebrates to be **bipedal**, or able to walk on two legs. Not all dinosaurs were bipedal, but they all evolved from an ancestor that was.

Scientists also look at a fossil's hand bones to identify which are dinosaurs and which aren't. Dinosaurs' thumbs were set at a different angle from the rest of their fingers. This meant that they could grip things by closing their hands, allowing their thumb and fingers to meet.

Another thing that helps scientists identify dinosaurs is their hips. In most living animals, the place where the bone of the thigh meets the hip socket is a solid piece of bone. In dinosaurs, the inside of the hip socket is made of a soft tissue called cartilage. No one knows why dinosaurs were made this way—perhaps it made it easier to walk—but it is an important difference between them and other animals.

The hip bone does more than identify whether a fossil is from a dinosaur. It also helps narrow down what kind of dinosaur it was. In 1887, a British scientist named Harry Seeley divided the dinosaur family tree into two different branches: Saurischia—or "lizard-hipped" dinosaurs—and Ornithischia—or "bird-hipped" dinosaurs. These are actually misleading names, since lizards and birds didn't exist before dinosaurs. They both evolved from dinosaur ancestors. Interestingly enough, birds actually descended from the lizard-hipped Saurischians!

THE SAURISCHIANS

The **Saurischians** are a strange bunch. They are divided into two groups: giant meat-eating dinosaurs called **theropods** which

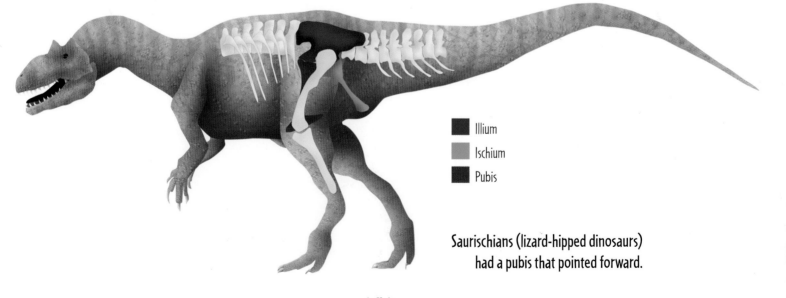

■ Illium
■ Ischium
■ Pubis

Saurischians (lizard-hipped dinosaurs)
had a pubis that pointed forward.

walked on two three-toed feet—like *Tyrannosaurus rex*, *Velociraptor*, and *Eoraptor*—and long-necked, plant-eating dinosaurs called **sauropodomorphs**—like *Apatosaurus* and *Diplodocus*. In fact, the biggest known dinosaur and the smallest known dinosaur are both Saurischians. So how could such different types of dinosaurs be grouped together?

Though it may not seem likely, the theropods and sauropodomorphs had more in common than you'd think. They all had long necks that moved easily and hands with asymmetrical fingers capable of grasping things. Their vertebrae—the bones that made up their backbones—were made up of many hollow cavities. And of course, all Saurischians had similar hip bones, with a bone called the pubis that pointed forward.

THE ORNITHISCHIANS

The **Ornithischians** were no less special than the Saurischians. In fact, some of the most well-known dinosaurs were Ornithischians: *Stegosaurus*, *Ankylosaurus*, *Triceratops*, *Hadrosaurus*, and *Iguanodon*. Ornithischians had a pubis that pointed down and toward the tail, and their pelvises were wider than those of the Saurischians. This made the Ornithischians more stable when they walked.

Ornithischians were **herbivores**. That means they ate plants. These dinosaurs had an extra bone in the front of their lower jaw that formed a sort of beak structure. The Ornithischians used

Velociraptors were meat-eating dinosaurs known as theropods.

this beak to clip off plant material to eat. Ornithischians were smaller than the massive sauropodomorphs, which meant these plant eaters were often **prey** for the meat-eating theropods.

Ornithischians (bird-hipped dinosaurs) had a pubis that pointed down.

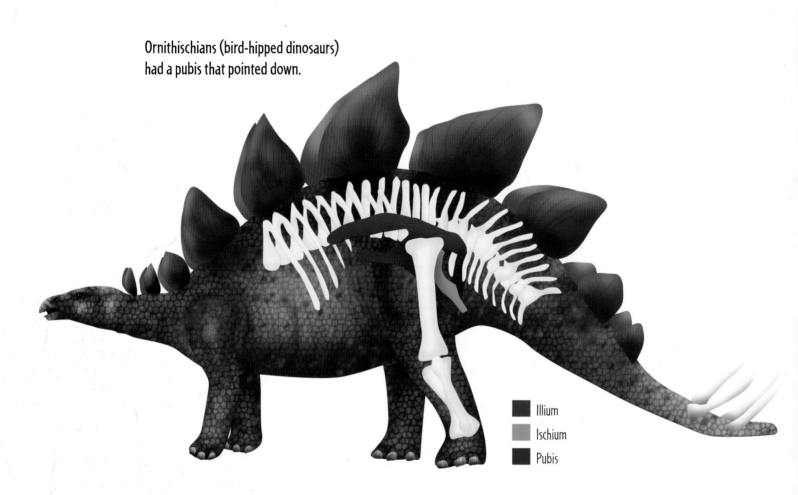

Illium
Ischium
Pubis

Stegosaurus was a plant-eating dinosaur known as an Ornithischian.

What Came First, the Dino or the Egg?

THERE AREN'T MANY THINGS that scientists can say with one hundred percent certainty about dinosaur babies. But that doesn't mean we don't know some things. In fact, there is at least one indisputable fact about baby dinosaurs: They all hatched from eggs.

As we know, all dinosaurs lived on land. These ancient animals laid their eggs on land, too. Scientists have found fossilized eggs all over the world that belong to every kind of dinosaur.

The eggs may be spherical in shape, elongated ovals with symmetrical ends, or more chicken-egg shaped, with one end of the oval being smaller than the other. The eggs come in many different shapes, and the brittle, easily broken shells have textures ranging from smooth to wrinkled to bumpy.

Scientists now know that certain types of dinosaurs laid eggs of particular shapes or textures. This information helps link new dinosaur egg discoveries to known species. For example, paleontologists have noticed that when a dinosaur egg is elongated, it usually belongs to a theropod. If the egg is shaped like a sphere, it probably came from a **sauropod** or Ornithischian.

Of course, shape can sometimes be deceiving. In 1981, a strange new dinosaur called *Therizinosaurus* was discovered. It had a long neck, a wide torso, and hind feet with four toes. Its hip bone pointed backward and reminded paleontologists at first of a "bird-hipped" Ornithischian. But its claws and hands were more like that of a theropod.

A three-and-a-half-inch round egg was found with what appeared to be a baby *Therizinosaurus* inside. This creature was

Dinosaur eggs came in all shapes and sizes.

Dendroolithus
(Sauropods, Ornithopods)

Faveloloolithus (Sauropods)

Elongatoolithidus (Theropods)

Spheroolithus (Ornithopods)

Megaloolithus (Sauropods)

curled up in a fetal position. Interestingly, an eighteen-inch elongated egg was also discovered with what appeared to be a *Therizinosaurus* inside. Scientists named this unhatched dinosaur Baby Louie! The two eggs were different sizes and shapes, and had different textures. The babies inside had different skin patterns and coloration, and were different sizes, but otherwise looked strikingly similar.

As more eggs are discovered and examined, especially from the site where Baby Louie was found, scientists hope to have a better understanding of which dinosaurs these eggs really came from. Maybe they are the same species, and maybe they aren't. Until we know for sure, paleontologists must acknowledge the possibility that egg shape doesn't tell us as much as we once thought.

As the *Therizinosaurus* eggs show, dinosaur eggs not only come in many different shapes, but in different sizes as well. The biggest dinosaur eggs ever found also happen to be the first dinosaur eggs to be discovered. In 1869, Philippe Matheron found egg fragments in Rognac, France, near the bones of a large plant-eating sauropod called *Hypselosaurus priscus*. (At the time, though, *Hypselosaurus* was not known to be a dinosaur.) The eggs were one foot long and ten inches wide, and could hold about half a gallon of **embryo** material. Scientists estimate that the eggs could have weighed up to 15.5 pounds before they hatched. (Interestingly enough, the *Hypsel-*

Therizinosaurus had a long neck, long torso, and hind feet with four toes.

osaurus eggs, although large in comparison to something like a chicken egg, were nowhere near the size of the eggs laid by the extinct elephant bird of Madagascar, which laid 2.4-gallon eggs—almost five times bigger than *Hypselosaurus*.)

The smallest dinosaur eggs were discovered in 1979, more than a hundred years after the *Hypselosaurus* discovery. They came from a small, plant-eating species called *Mussaurus* ("mouse reptile"). These eggs were about one inch long. The hatchlings were around eight inches long including a long tail. With its tail curled up, a baby *Mussaurus* could be held comfortably in a human's hand.

Mice are small animals as adults, and their babies are tiny. Elephants are huge animals, and their babies are pretty big. Human adults are in between, and so are our babies. But scientists have learned an important fact from studying dinosaur eggs: No matter how huge they grew, the babies all started out fairly small. Just take a look for yourself:

Dinosaur	Length as an Adult	Egg Size	Length of Hatchling
Hypselosaurus	27 feet	1 foot long, 10 inches wide	Unknown
Protoceratops	6 feet	6-8 inches long	4-6 inches
Camptosaurus	16 feet	Unknown	9-10 inches
Oviraptor	8 feet	6 inches long	8 inches
Mussaurus	10 feet	1 inch long	8 inches
Maiasaura	25-30 feet	8 inches long	14 inches
Hypsilophodontids	7 feet	6 inches long	Unknown

MODERN MEDICINE

Although scientists can sometimes use an egg's shape, texture, and size to determine what species a particular dinosaur egg belongs to, it is still no easy task to learn about how these creatures grew. For many years, it was difficult to study the remains of the dinosaur embryos inside fossilized eggs. (An embryo is a baby forming in an egg.) Recently, however, scientists have begun to use advanced medical technologies to study dinosaur embryos. Using X-rays—the same thing doctors use to study human bones—scientists in Montana were able to scan and study nineteen fossilized embryos from 75-million-year-old dinosaurs. The information they learned from the X-rays, combined with adult bones found near the nest, led to the classification of a new genus and species of the Hypsilophodontid family, which scientists called *Orodromeus makelai*. *Orodromeus*, which means "mountain runner," prob-

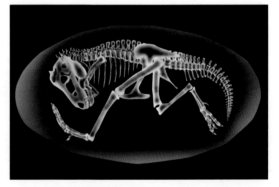

ably grew to about eight feet in length. Because of its long thighs, scientists think that it was a very fast runner.

In another case of using current technology, scientists used a CAT scan to study an egg found near the twenty-foot-high bones of an *Allosaurus* fossil. They

X-rays help scientists to determine what species a dinosaur inside an egg is.

assumed the egg was an *Allosaurus* egg, but wanted to study it more carefully. CAT scans use X-rays and computers to generate 3-D images of internal structures. The CAT scan showed that there was probably a very young embryo inside the egg, maybe three or four days old. What is especially exciting about this is that scientists believe that this egg probably had not been laid yet—it had fossilized while still inside the mother!

THE VALUE OF AN EGGSHELL

Dinosaur eggs are an *egg*-citing find, since they can tell us a lot about dinosaur babies and how they developed. But even when only eggshells are left behind, they are excellent sources of information. By studying the chemicals that make up eggshells, scientists can learn about what dinosaurs ate and drank in the weeks before the egg was laid.

Every type of water has its own mix of minerals, like magnesium, strontium, and iron. Scientists can measure the amounts of different minerals in a sample of water and determine whether it is rainwater, spring water, swamp water, or river water. Scientists already know that chickens that drink expensive mineral water lay chemically different eggs than those that drink tap water. Similarly, eggshells from dinosaurs that drank spring water are chemically different than eggshells from animals that drank swamp water. As it turns out, the mix of minerals remains unchanged as water passes through an animal's digestive system and when it is deposited in an eggshell.

Isabelle Cojan is a scientist in Paris. She and her colleagues studied eggshells found in two different parts of Aix en Provence, France—one area that used to be a floodplain and another area that used to be a forest. She explains, "Eggs form over a short period of time, so they provide us with an instant picture of animal conditions."

Cojan's analysis of fossilized eggshells from the floodplain suggested that the dinosaurs that laid eggs there drank water from local rivers. Analysis of eggshells from the forest, on the other hand, showed that the dinosaurs that laid eggs there drank water that had circulated through the rocks. Though the two areas were relatively close, it seems from these results that dinosaurs tended to stay in their own territory. Says Cojan, "The distinctive differences indicate that the dinosaurs settled for some time at the places where they laid their eggs, and that migration was limited."

Eggshells can't tell the whole story, but as Cojan learned, they can help us understand a lot more than just how eggs hatched.

HATCHING THE BABIES

Most modern-day birds build a nest, lay their eggs, and then sit on the eggs until they hatch. This is called brooding. Although there is evidence that some dinosaurs did the same thing, it is clear that

not all dinosaurs did so. After all, when you weigh four tons (like the duck-billed dinosaur called *Maiasaura*), there's a good chance that trying to care for the eggs by brooding them will actually crush them. Instead, dinosaurs like *Maiasaura* probably padded their nests with rotting plant materials, much like modern-day crocodiles do. As these materials decomposed, they released heat—enough to keep the eggs in the nest warm until they hatched.

So how did dinosaur eggs actually hatch? Adult crocodiles use their jaws to gently crack open their eggs when they are ready to hatch. A hatchling crocodile also has an egg tooth (a sharp bit of tissue that sticks out from its head) to help it crack through the shell. Some birds have an egg tooth, too, while other birds are known to break their way out of the eggshell using the strength of their legs. With dinosaur eggs, of course, we cannot be sure what the hatchlings did. But there are some things that the evidence they left behind can tell us.

Scientists think that dinosaur babies likely pushed their way through the eggshell using their legs. Whenever a hatched, fossilized egg has been found, the opening has been on the top. This suggests that the dinosaur babies pushed their way up to get through the shell. They may have used an egg tooth to crack the shell, like birds do, but there is no evidence of this yet.

But how can we tell the difference between eggs that hatched and those that were trampled or eaten by a predator? When an

Dinosaurs like *Maiasaura* probably padded their nests with plants.

egg hatched, no eggshell fragments are found inside the remaining shell. When an egg was damaged before hatching, fragments of eggshell can be found inside the remaining shell, suggesting the predator pushed on the egg.

YOU GIVE OVIRAPTOR A BAD NAME

Just finding an egg isn't enough to learn about a dinosaur's childhood. After all, scientists first have to identify what kind of egg they've found—and that can be a bigger challenge than finding the egg in the first place. Paleontologists face several problems when identifying eggs. The bones of a forming dinosaur baby are not well developed. After millions of years, there is often little evidence left behind in a fossilized egg. Furthermore, a baby may not resemble the adult dinosaur at all. If the fossil of an adult isn't found near the egg or nest, it is almost impossible to definitively name the species.

Even when adult fossils *are* found near eggs, identification is not foolproof. One of the most famous dinosaur fossil discoveries was made by a paleontologist named Roy Chapman Andrews in the Gobi Desert of Mongolia in the 1920s. (Andrews was considered so adventurous that Indiana Jones was modeled on him.) On this excursion, Andrews identified many new species of dinosaurs—and made a huge case of mistaken identity.

One of the new species found on Andrews's expedition was

Scientists think dinosaurs pushed their way
out of their shells with their legs.

discovered by his photographer, James B. Shackleford. This creature, a plant eater that had a neck frill and a massive frontal beak, was named *Protoceratops*, meaning "first horned face." Over seventy *Protoceratops* specimens were located nearby, and later a nest of eggs was also found. Although the bones of a different dinosaur were found on top of the nest, there were so many *Protoceratops* around that the scientists assumed the eggs belonged to *Protoceratops*. The other dinosaur seemed to be a meat eater, and it made sense that it was there to steal and eat the *Protoceratops* eggs. Scientists assumed that it was likely killed where it stood by an angry *Protoceratops* parent. The second dinosaur was named *Oviraptor philoceratops*, "the egg stealer with a love of ceratops eggs."

For decades, *Oviraptor* was known as the egg thief. But in 1995, Dr. Philip Currie and his team of scientists found another Mongolian nest of dinosaur eggs with another *Oviraptor* sitting on top of the nest. The next year, a dinosaur skeleton was found inside one of the Mongolian eggs. To everyone's surprise, the bones belonged to an *Oviraptor*, not to a *Protoceratops*.

All of a sudden, it was clear that *Oviraptor* was far from being an egg thief. Actually, the animals found on the nests were now thought to be a mother or father *Oviraptor* protecting its nest by sitting on the eggs. Not only did this finding prove that *Oviraptor* had been given a bad rap for too many years, it showed that these dinosaurs were probably very good parents. The fossil of the adult

Protoceratops had a neck frill and a massive front beak.

Oviraptor had its legs folded under its body, and its forelimbs were encircling a clutch of at least fifteen eggs. This is the strongest piece of evidence to date that some dinosaurs sat on their eggs like modern birds do. It is possible that the parent *Oviraptor* was trying to shield the nest from a severe sandstorm, a common occurrence in the Gobi Desert, that buried the family group and preserved them in the pose in which they were discovered.

A CRÈCHE OF PARROT LIZARDS

Finding an adult dinosaur skeleton brooding its nest of fossilized eggs is an excellent clue about dinosaur parenting techniques. But finding an adult in close proximity to young dinosaurs provides an even better look at how dinosaurs raised their babies. In 2004, scientists Qingjin Meng and his team found the fossilized remains of an adult *Psittacosaurus* (meaning "parrot lizard"), a plant-eating dinosaur that measured around three feet long. *Psittacosaurus* had a parrot-like beak (which is what gave them their name) and cheek horns.

What was especially interesting about the *Psittacosaurus* discovery was that the adult was found surrounded by thirty-four juveniles. What's more, all of the young dinosaurs were found within an area of half a square meter. The bodies were clustered together with their heads raised and their legs tucked under their bodies. This suggests that they were buried together while still alive—which

Scientists think *Oviraptor* brooded its eggs.

also means that the adult was likely caring for the young dinosaurs in some way. After all, it seems unlikely that so many juveniles would have accidentally been caught near the adult during whatever catastrophe caused their deaths.

The discovery of the *Psittacosaurus* fossils taught scientists other things, too. The juveniles that were found with the adult were not newly hatched babies. Instead, they were around twenty centimeters long, far bigger than hatchlings. This tells scientists that the adult dinosaur was probably responsible for taking care of the young for quite some time.

The uniform size of the young *Psittacosauruses* suggests that they were all from the same brood, but scientists are not sure whether they were all part of the same family. But why would juvenile dinosaurs congregate around an adult that was not their parent? One possible answer is that *Psittacosaurus* was a lot like modern-day Emperor penguins. The eggs of all the Emperor penguins in a colony hatch around the same time, one chick per pair of parents. Rather than every parent being responsible for child care at all times, these penguins choose a few adults to take care of a crèche, or group of chicks from several different families. This allows the other adults to search for food and keep their eyes out for predators. It is possible that the thirty-four *Psittacosaurus* juveniles made up a crèche, and that these dinosaurs parented in a way similar to Emperor penguins.

One adult *Psittacosaurus* may have been responsible for juveniles from several families.

FIERCE OR FEEBLE?

Studying eggshells and the skeletons of dinosaur fetuses tells scientists more than how dinosaurs developed and where they lived. It also helps them to find valuable clues about what kind of parenting the baby dinosaurs needed. For example, the *Orodromeus* fetuses found in Montana had well-formed joints made out of hardened cartilage. This suggests that these dinosaur babies developed very quickly and were likely able to leave their nests and take care of themselves almost immediately. Scientists believe that other dinosaurs, like the hadrosaurid, were slow to develop. Their bones at birth might have been too weak for the babies to be able to walk, leaving them dependent on their parents for care. It is possible that some hadrosaurids stayed in the nest for up to a year after hatching.

Were Dinosaurs Good Parents?

IT IS DIFFICULT ENOUGH to determine whether dinosaurs took care of their eggs before hatching, but figuring out whether dinosaurs were good parents to their hatchlings is almost impossible to do with any kind of certainty. It is hard to find a fossil record of a mother dinosaur teaching a hatchling to walk while navigating difficult terrain, or of a father dinosaur teaching a juvenile to hunt. Other things, like whether parent dinosaurs took care of sick or wounded young, or rewarded good behavior with extra helpings of *Stegosaurus* ribs, are equally difficult to find evidence of. So the ways in which paleontologists make educated guesses about dinosaur parenting is a painstaking process involving every piece of data that can be found.

In fact, figuring out parental care in dinosaurs is a main area of dinosaur research these days. But why would dinosaurs take care of their children at all? Not all modern-day animals do so.

Several animals, like sea turtles and some sharks, lay eggs and never look back. These animals leave their babies to fend for themselves. Scientists used to believe that dinosaurs were similar—that they just laid their eggs and went on their merry ways. But based on new discoveries, scientists now believe that there was some type of parental care, at least in some dinosaurs.

One reason to take care of babies is survival of the species. Scientists now know that dinosaurs usually laid lots of eggs at once, because eggs are usually found in groups, or clutches. The largest number of eggs thought to be laid at one time is twenty, from a sauropod called *Megaloolithus*. (Interestingly, the smallest number of eggs thought to be laid at one time, one, is also from a *Megaloolithus*, though it is possible these were rejected eggs rather than a small breeding year.) The reason to lay so many eggs at once is to improve the chances that some of the babies will survive to adulthood. We see this behavior in modern-day sea turtles, which lay up to two hundred eggs at a time. A good number of those eggs will be eaten by predators before hatching, and most of the hatchlings won't survive the first year of life. But a large clutch size ensures that enough turtles grow up to reproduce and keep the species going.

One way to improve survival of the young is parental protection. A baby dinosaur of almost any species would have made an easy meal for a predator. Even in the cases where the babies were

Some dinosaurs, like the *Triceratops*, protected their young from predators.

mobile, they certainly couldn't fight for survival against a much bigger hunter, and may not have been able to outrun one, either. So it was up to the parent to keep the baby safe.

HABITS OF HADROSAURIDS AND OTHER HERBIVORES

When you think of the rock stars of the dinosaur world, it is usually the giant **carnivores** that get all the media attention. But when it comes to understanding dinosaurs, it is often the gentle giants like *Apatosaurus*, *Maiasaurus*, and *Hadrosaurus* that scientists know the most about. These herbivores often lived in herds of hundreds. That means that they left a lot of fossil evidence behind on giant bone beds containing adults, juveniles, and babies. It also means that scientists have been able to study these dinosaurs at many points of their lives—from babies to teenagers to adults—allowing them to learn a great deal about how dinosaurs parented their young.

Hadrosaurids in particular are one of the best-studied dinosaurs in the world. Whole herds of these dinosaurs have been found in South America, Europe, Asia, and Antarctica. "Hadrosaurid" is the scientific name for duck-billed dinosaurs, which were the last type of two-legged, plant-eating dinosaurs with beaks to evolve. It was their beaks—the broad and rounded end of the snout that resembled the bill of a duck—that gave hadrosaurids their nickname. There were two types of hadrosaurids: the Hadrosaurines

Scientists know more about herbivores than any other kind of dinosaur.

and the Lambeosaurines. Examples of Hadrosaurines include *Hadrosaurus*, *Prosaurolophus*, and *Maiasaura*. These dinosaurs had big noses and broad snouts. The Lambeosaurines looked a lot like the Hadrosaurines, but were identified as their own group by the hollow crests they had sticking out of the backs of their skulls. The crest could look like a tube, as in *Parasaurolophus*, or like a helmet, as in *Lambeosaurus* and *Hypacrosaurus*.

Lambeosaurines were not born with their distinctive crests. Instead, the crest grew as the animal got older, starting as a bump on the front of the face. With age, the crest became more pronounced and visible. In fact, because Lambeosaurines of different ages looked nothing like one another, scientists mistakenly labeled adults, juveniles, and babies as different species.

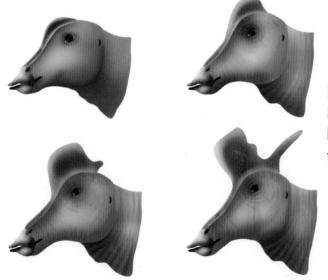

Lambeosaurines had crests that grew larger the older they got.

Lambeosaurines had duck-billed beaks and hollow crests on the tops of their heads.

GOOD MOTHER LIZARDS

One of the most famous hadrosaurids was found in Montana and named by John Horner. In 1978, Horner walked into a small rock shop owned by Marion Brandvold. She showed him a coffee can filled with fossilized bones, which Horner almost immediately recognized as baby dinosaur bones. Brandvold led Horner to the site where she and her son had discovered the bones. After Horner and his team did some further excavations, they realized that they had found one of the most important dinosaur sites in North America, later named "Egg Mountain."

There were two very significant discoveries made at Egg Mountain. First, the baby dinosaur bones belonged to an entirely new species of dinosaur that Horner named *Maiasaura*, meaning "good mother lizard." Horner estimated that there were the remains of ten thousand *Maiasauras* on Egg Mountain. Second, Egg Mountain was the first site on earth where dinosaur nests were found not just with fossilized eggs in them, but with fossilized babies.

Horner picked the name *Maiasaura* because of the evidence he found concerning the babies on Egg Mountain. When the bones of the baby *Maiasauras* were examined, it was discovered that the joints of the knees may not have been strong enough to support the weight of the babies' bodies. This means the babies might not have been able to walk on their own, and were therefore unable to search for food by themselves. Horner found pieces of fossil-

Scientists believe that adult *Maiasauras* brought food back to the nest for their babies.

ized eggshell inside the nests that were so small, he concluded they must have been trampled. This suggested that the babies stayed in the nest for quite some time—which might have had the added benefit of preventing the sixteen-inch hatchlings from being trampled by the thirty-foot adults. Also, the babies' teeth showed signs of wear. Since they could not leave the nest to get food, Horner believed it only made sense that adult *Maiasauras* were bringing food back to their babies.

A BABY'S PLACE

Not all scientists agree with the interpretation that *Maiasaura* babies needed parental care. Scientists Nicholas Geist and Terry Jones examined the hip and knee bones of different birds and alligators. They compared the hip bones and knee joints of *Maiasaura* to that of modern-day birds and alligators, which don't need parental care. The *Maiasaura* hips were at least as well-developed as the birds', and the knee joints were no weaker than the birds' or alligators'. This might mean that *Maiasaura* babies did not need care from their parents as Horner believed.

Regardless of how the bone evidence is interpreted, it is clear that baby *Maiasauras* congregated together after birth, possibly to look out for one another. When scientists have found bone beds containing adult *Maiasaura* bones, the smallest bones nearby were about half the size of the largest adult. This suggests that the very young dinosaurs stayed separate from the adults and only joined the main herd after they had grown to a certain size.

Why would babies and adults stay separate? One possibility is speed. Adult hadrosaurids traveled far and wide. Their long legs made this easy. Baby hadrosaurids, on the other hand, had much shorter legs and probably would have had a hard time keeping up. Each step taken by an adult, twenty-three-foot-long hadrosaurid would have been about eight feet long. But a twenty-six-inch baby hadrosaurid would have only taken a 12.5-inch step, meaning

Baby hadrosaurids had small legs, and would have had a hard time keeping up with adults.

that for every adult step, the poor baby would have had to run to take seven or eight. All that running would have been too tiring to keep up for long. So it seems likely that baby hadrosaurids banded together with their brothers and sisters and any others of the same age to form a "newborn posse," separate from the moms and dads.

Of course, there is no proof that all dinosaurs kept the babies away from the older members of a herd. In fact, the younger members of *Apatosaurus* herds probably stayed close to the adults at all times. Adult *Apatosauruses* were so large that they did not have many enemies, but the younger dinosaurs would have been easy pickings for gigantic predators like *Allosaurus*. Scientists have

discovered a set of dinosaur tracks in Texas that appears to show a herd of sauropods traveling together, with adult tracks on the outside of the group and younger dinosaurs in the center. The young probably stayed close to adults so that the massive size of the adults would cause a predator to think twice before attacking.

FOOTPRINTS IN THE SAND

Sometimes the only clues that a paleontologist needs to learn about dinosaur families are footprints. Scientists believe that there may have been a really hot dinosaur hangout around 190 million years ago in what is now the Vermilion Cliffs National Monument along the Arizona-Utah border. This is based on more than one thousand footprints and tail-drag marks preserved on the ground.

Scientists have found four distinct types of tracks at the site. The ten- to sixteen-inch-long footprints with three toes and a heel were likely made by a dinosaur like *T. rex*, but smaller, that walked upright. The four- to seven-inch-long, three-toed footprints were left by dinosaurs that stood only a few feet tall. Another kind of three-toed footprint, commonly seven to ten inches long, was probably left by dinosaurs that were between six and thirteen feet in length. Lastly, the circular footprints, mostly six to eleven inches long, which had tail-drag marks associated with them, were probably left by very large dinosaurs that walked on four legs, like sauropods.

Large sauropods protected their young by walking on the outside of their packs, shielding the smaller pack members from predators.

Scientists discovered four different kinds of footprints at the Vermilion Cliffs National Monument.

The different kinds of tracks suggest that there was more than just one type of dinosaur congregating in the area. Some of these tracks were even as small as one inch long. One scientist at the University of Utah, Winston Seiler, said, "The different size tracks may tell us that we are seeing mothers walking around with babies." Without skeletons, we can't be sure, but this is interesting possible evidence of parental care.

SIZE MATTERS

We know that dinosaur hatchlings were very, very small compared to many of the humongous adult skeletons that have been found. Interestingly, scientists have determined that there is a mathematical formula that can be used to guess the size of a hatchling. First, you figure out what the average size of an adult of the species is in millimeters. Then you use this formula:

$$\text{Size of the hatchling in millimeters} = 12.5 \times (\text{average size of the adult in millimeters})^{0.38}$$

This may seem like complicated math, but it is very useful when scientists find young skeletons. For example, take a skeleton from a small *Maiasaura* that was 300 millimeters (11.8 inches) long. An adult *Maiasaura* is about seven meters, or 7,000 millimeters (22.9 feet) long. Using the mathematical formula, scientists can calculate that a hatchling should be 360 millimeters (14 inches) long. That means the skeleton found was likely an embryo instead of a hatchling. As more and more young dinosaur remains are uncovered, it is important that scientists have this way to separate the hatchlings from the not-yet-hatched.

HOW DID YOUR DINO GROW?

An important part of growing up is, well, growing bigger. And dinosaurs certainly grew to be gigantic! But even species that were the same size as adults often had very different growth patterns.

Everyone knows that kids go through growth spurts, and of course, dinosaurs did as well. For many years, scientists thought that dinosaurs may have grown in a similar way to reptiles. These creatures grow slowly, but continue to grow for pretty much their whole lives. A fifty-year-old crocodile is bigger than a twenty-year-old croc, but smaller than a seventy-year-old.

Other scientists, though, felt that dinosaurs probably grew in a more birdlike manner. Birds start growing as babies, then enter a phase of very rapid growth. When they reach adult size, they stop growing almost altogether. (Coincidentally, this is similar to the pattern that many mammals—including humans—follow. In larger mammals, though, the first two phases may be years long versus months long in most birds.)

Dr. Kristi Curry Rogers is one paleontologist who is interested in figuring out how quickly dinosaurs grew. She realized that if very large dinosaurs like *Apatosaurus* grew in a reptilelike pattern, it would take over a hundred years for them to reach the sizes that we've seen in fossils. That didn't make sense to her, so she explored the issue further.

Dr. Rogers realized that she could study the bones of a dinosaur under a microscope to learn about the animal's growth. In vertebrates, bones grow out and up—the same way that trees grow. Like in trees, where you can count the rings to calculate age, bones can

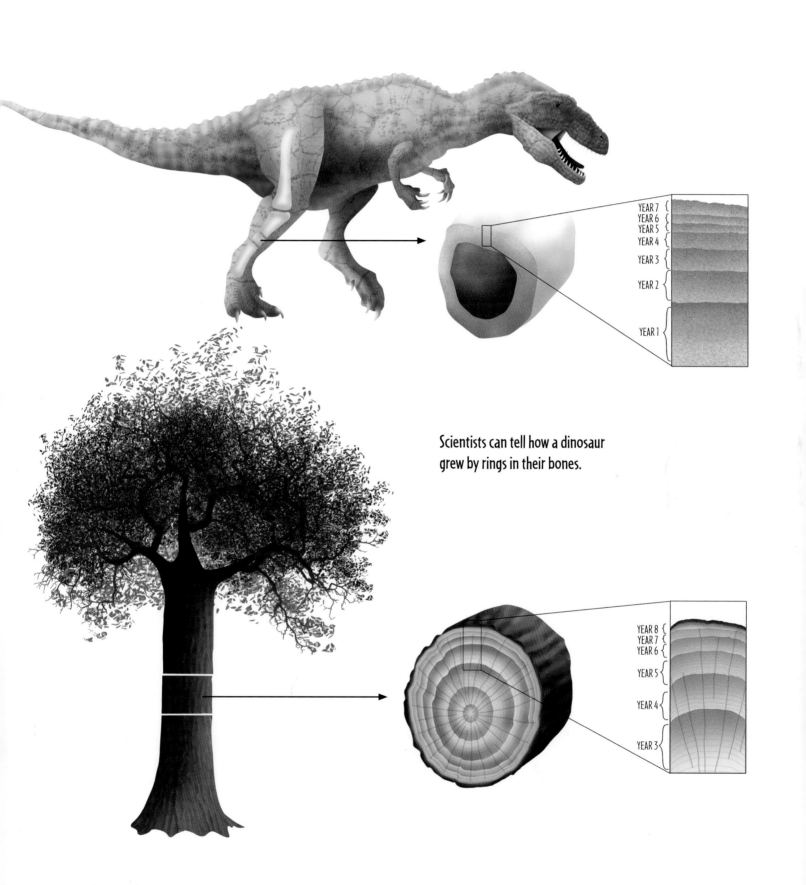

YEAR 7
YEAR 6
YEAR 5
YEAR 4
YEAR 3
YEAR 2
YEAR 1

Scientists can tell how a dinosaur grew by rings in their bones.

YEAR 8
YEAR 7
YEAR 6
YEAR 5
YEAR 4
YEAR 3

also leave rings behind as they grow. These growth rings, called lines of arrested growth (LAGs), are made up of proteins, minerals, and blood vessels.

Bones are made of a type of calcium that is deposited on a long, fiberlike protein called collagen. When an animal grows slowly, the collagen proteins lie parallel to one another and all of the calcium minerals point the same way. In a fast-growing animal, on the other hand, both the collagen and minerals form a disorganized, irregular layout. In addition, there are usually many more blood vessels in the bones of fast-growing animals than in slower growing ones.

Just because an animal grows rapidly doesn't mean that its growth rate is uniform. It is likely that dinosaurs alternated between periods of rapid growth and other phases of slower growth. This makes sense, in that animals grow faster when there is an abundance of food, like in spring and summer, and growth slows down when food is scarce, like in winter. Dr. Rogers found that *Apatosaurus* bones had disorganized proteins and minerals, but she did not find any growth rings in the bones. This not only meant that *Apatosaurus* grew very quickly, but that this dinosaur must have grown uniformly throughout the year, unaffected by seasons. Dr. Rogers was also able to calculate that instead of taking a hundred years to grow to full size, *Apatosaurus* was able to go from zero to thirty (thirty tons, that is) in only ten to twelve years.

MOM, DAD, OR UNCLE FILMORE: WHO DID BABY LOOK LIKE?

When people go to visit a new baby in the maternity ward, one of the first things they try to figure out is whether baby looks like Mommy or Daddy. When dinosaur babies are found, this is hard for scientists to do—so hard, in fact, that many dinosaur babies have been given different names than their parents because paleontologists could not tell that the grown-ups and babies were related from looking at them. As we learn more about baby dinosaurs, many of the previously found skeletons are being renamed.

One of the reasons that paleontologists made such *Apatosaurus*-sized mistakes was that, often, there were significant differences in the appearances of adult versus baby dinosaurs. Around the same time that scientists discovered the *Oviraptor* error, another case of mistaken identity was corrected. In 1993, David Varricchio found a clutch of fossilized eggs under the remains of an adult *Troodon*. The eggs strongly resembled what was then thought to be the eggs of a smaller, plant-eating dinosaur called *Orodromeus*. *Orodromeus* fossils had been found nearby, and after examining the embryos the scientists realized that they had fairly undeveloped teeth, markedly different from *Troodon*'s large, serrated teeth. At first, scientists believed they had found a *Troodon* caught in the act of trying to steal from an *Orodromeus* nest.

Because the *Oviraptor-Protoceratops* mix-up had been recently revealed, Varricchio was encouraged to dig a little deeper (so to speak) with the supposed *Orodromeus* eggs. When the embryos were compared to the remains of four *Troodons* ranging from half-grown to adult, it became clear that these eggs had been mislabeled. *Troodon* was no thief. Instead, it is possible that the adult *Troodon* found on the nest was brooding the eggs.

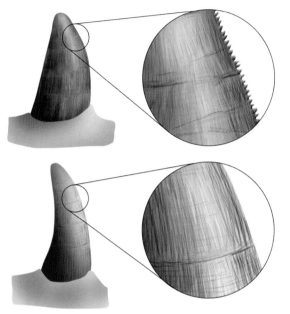

In an adult *Troodon*, the teeth are as sharp as steak knives. In

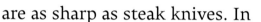

Troodon's teeth changed as it grew older.

Troodon embryos, on the other hand, the teeth look more like salad leaves. One hatchling *Troodon* was found with no teeth at all! Scientists had a similar problem with *Velociraptor*—an adult's teeth are thin, pointy, and serrated, while an embryo's teeth are pointed crowns that look like pegs.

Knowing that dinosaurs' teeth changed as they grew makes sense in light of what is known about modern lizards. Several lizards have small, pointy teeth as babies, but big, fat teeth as adults. Their diet changes as they grow, so their teeth change as well. This was probably true of dinosaurs, too.

Tooth shape was only one way in which dinosaur babies differed from their parents in appearance. The heads and bodies of adult ankylosaurs, for example, were covered in armored plates called scutes. In baby ankylosaurs, however, the scutes were smaller and less developed. In fact, babies had no scutes on their heads at all.

Appearance also affected how scientists labeled ceratopsids. The first ceratopsid skull to be found had three horns, two on the brow bone and one on the nose. This species was named *Triceratops*, which means "three-horned face." Later, many other ceratopsids were discovered, including *Diceratus* (which had two horns on its brow bone and a rounded stump where the nose horn should have

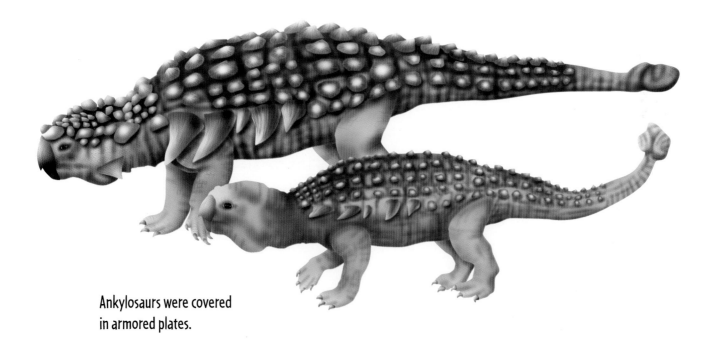

Ankylosaurs were covered
in armored plates.

been); *Styracosaurus* (which had four to six horns on its neck, one horn on each cheek, and a nose horn that could grow up to two feet long); and the largest ceratopsid of them all, *Pentaceratops* (which had five horns: two on the brow bone, one on the nose, and two pointing sideways under the eyes).

Despite the differences in the appearances of adult ceratopsids, scientists have discovered that all baby and young ceratopsids, no matter the species, pretty much looked the same! Early on, scientists didn't realize this, and so two types of ceratopsids were mistakenly named: *Brachyceratops*, which had small bumps on the brow bone instead of horns, and a single, thick, low horn on the nose; and *Monoclonius*, which had small bumps on the brow bone and a big horn on the nose. As it turns out, what scientists thought were *Brachyceratops* and *Monoclonius* species were actually just growth phases of other ceratopsids.

How did scientists figure this out? It started on a weekend trip to Pipestone Creek in Canada for a junior high school teacher named Al Lakusta. Lakusta had found some plant fossils in the creek bed on a previous trip, but when he returned he discovered fossilized rib fragments farther upstream. He climbed a steep slope and caught sight of even more bones—sun-bleached, but recognizable as rib bones and vertebrae.

When the site that Lakusta found was excavated, scientists counted more than 3,500 bones, making it the second-largest

Because ceratopsids looked different at different ages, many were initially mislabeled by scientists.

Baby allosaurs looked like small versions of adults.

dinosaur fossil site in North America. The bones were from an entire herd of ceratopsids known as *Pachyrhinosaurus*, the "thick-nosed reptile." Scientists think that the herd might have been on a migration path across a river when they drowned in flood as a group.

Among the *Pachyrhinosaurus* bones were skulls that resembled *Brachyceratops* and *Monoclonius*. It made less sense that different species would be traveling together than that a group of the same species of different ages had been found. This led scientists to realize that ceratopsids changed in appearance as they grew, and that it was likely that these dinosaurs, at least, lived in large family groups. This probably meant that they found food and ate together, and that they looked out for one another when predators were nearby. As the younger ceratopsids would have been less experienced in food gathering and predator spotting, it is probable that their parents took responsibility for most of these tasks—and therefore took responsibility, at least in part, for caring for the young in the herd.

Unlike ceratopsids, there were some dinosaur species where the babies looked like Mom and Dad. They were essentially miniatures of the adults. In 2005, paleontologist Dr. Oliver Rauhut discovered that baby *Allosauruses* looked a lot like adult *Allosauruses*, except that they were probably "cuter." What does that mean? The babies had large heads compared to the size of their bodies, and oversized eyes. These together would have given the babies that puppy-dog-eyes look that is so successful in generating sympathy and concern for, well, puppy dogs. Whether the puppy-dog eyes worked on *Allosaurus* parents is unknown, but it's possible that being cute was one way that baby *Allosauruses* guaranteed they would be cared for.

THE OLDEST EVIDENCE

Over the past few years, scientists have found more evidence of helpless dinosaur babies that had to be cared for by adults. In

2005, Dr. Robert Reisz and his team of scientists announced that they had possession of the oldest dinosaur eggs ever found. While digging in South Africa in 1978, they found 190-million-year-old unhatched eggs from a *Massospondylus*, an early sauropod related to giants like *Apatosaurus*. It took until 2005 to completely explore these eggs. What the scientists found inside were fully developed embryos that were ready to hatch. (They also found egg fragments around the site, which makes it likely that at least one of the eggs *did* hatch.) The embryos did not have any teeth, so the hatchlings could not have bitten growing plants for food. According to Dr. Reisz, this means that the mother *Massospondylus* must have fed her babies—making this is the oldest evidence of parental care ever found.

Another interesting thing about Dr. Reisz's findings was that the dinosaur embryos inside the eggs looked nothing like their parents. Adult *Massospondylus* specimens walked on two legs and were fairly slender. The babies, on the other hand, had overly-large heads and small pelvises. As most of the muscles used for walking would be in the pelvis, the babies were probably unable to move around. This is further evidence that adults brought food to the babies. Scientists believe that *Massospondylus* babies started out as **quadrupeds** (animals that walk on four legs) and eventually learned to walk on two legs. This may seem strange, until you realize that there is at least one other fairly successful species of

Baby *Massospondylus* had no teeth, so they couldn't eat without help from an adult.

animal in which the babies crawl on all fours but the adults walk on two feet. What species? Humans, of course.

HERBIVORE-ONLY HERDS?

Were the plant eaters the only ones to live in groups? For a long time, scientists might have said yes. Until recently it was widely believed that the massive meat eaters like *T. rex* were loners, living and hunting by themselves. In 1995, however, paleontologists found hundreds of bones in 100-million-year-old sandstone near Pala Huincul in Argentina. They realized that the bones were from a new species of meat-eating dinosaur, one that was similar in size to—if not bigger than—*T. rex*. They named this new species *Mapusaurus roseae*.

Since so many *Mapusauruses* were found together, scientists believe it is likely that these dinosaurs lived and hunted in a pack. Interestingly enough, there were fossils from dinosaurs of vastly different sizes—little babies, mid-sized "teenagers," and full-grown adults—buried in the same place, which suggests that the pack may have been a family. Some scientists believe that these dinosaurs may have hunted in family packs, with the smaller, faster juveniles chasing prey into the jaws of the more powerful adult dinosaurs. In fact, a *Mapusaurus* family hunting together might have been able to successfully take down *Argentinosaurus*, which at 132-feet-long was the largest dinosaur to walk the earth.

Mapusaurus families may have hunted in packs.

MONSTROUS MOMS AND DANGEROUS DADS

Between sixty-five and seventy million years ago, a type of thero-pod called *Majungasaurus* lived in Madagascar. *Majungasaurus* was a predator with a short but powerful snout. Adult *Majungasau-ruses* were the largest predators in their surroundings and almost anyone was fair game for a meal—including junior.

How do we know this? In 2003, Dr. Rogers and her colleagues reported that they had discovered many *Majungasaurus* bones in Madagascar with tooth marks that matched tooth marks found on sauropod bones in the area. The tooth marks were the same size as *Majungasaurus* teeth, and were spaced in the same way as teeth in *Majungasaurus* jaws. This made it pretty clear that some *Majungasauruses* were feeding on other *Majungasauruses*. Scientists don't know if *Majungasauruses* hunted other members of its own species or merely scavenged dead bodies, and it is unlikely that we can answer that question. But if *Majungasaurus* was anything like the modern-day Komodo dragon, cannibalism is a distinct possi-bility. Komodo dragons are known to kill each other when trying to compete for the same piece of meat, and once a rival is dead, the winner is known to feast on the remains.

Majungasaurus may have fed on other members of its species.

The Case of the Lizard King

POSSIBLY THE MOST FAMOUS dinosaur in the world is the terrible *Tyrannosaurus rex*. He had a powerful jaws, massive teeth, and long, speedy legs. In other words, he was built to be the perfect predator. But how did these creatures go from harmless eggs to universal tyrants?

Scientists have some ideas about how *T. rexes* grew and developed. For example, we know that baby *T. rexes* were born with long snouts and large teeth, which might mean that they were able to hunt independently from birth. The discovery of almost-complete juvenile *T. rex* skeletons have helped us better understand this phase of the *Tyrannosaurus rex*'s life.

THE CLEVELAND SKULL

Even when scientists do not have an entire skeleton to study, they can learn valuable things about a dinosaur from certain bones.

T. rex families lived together.

In the Cleveland Museum of Natural History, there is a twenty-three-inch skull that scientists first though belonged to a pygmy dinosaur, one that had grown to adulthood but had stopped growing bigger somewhere along the way. Adult *T. rexes* had teeth that stuck out of their mouths and thick, knobby skulls. The Cleveland skull was small and almost delicate. Its teeth were shorter and narrower than an adult *T. rexe's* would have been, and it had more of them. Also, the Cleveland skull was sleek, whereas an adult *T. rex* had a horn above and behind its eyes.

The Cleveland Museum of Natural History has a twenty-three-inch *T. rex* skull.

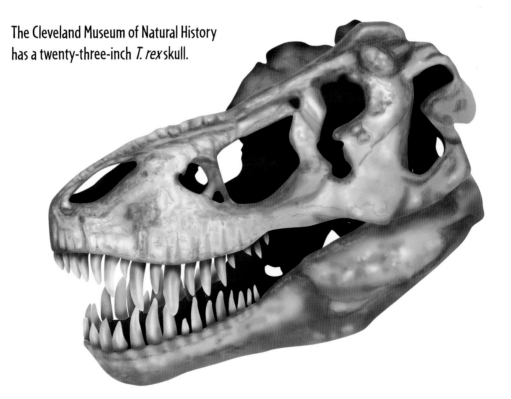

Dr. Thomas Carr compared the Cleveland skull to that of an adult *T. rex* and a juvenile dinosaur related to *T. rex*, *Albertosaurus*. He found that there were similarities between the Cleveland skull and the *T. rex* skull, but there were also similarities between the Cleveland skull and the juvenile *Albertosaurus*. Eventually, Dr. Carr realized that the Cleveland skull was not from a pygmy dinosaur. Instead, it was a juvenile *T. rex*.

Dr. Carr's findings give more evidence about the way *T. rexes* developed. As they got older, *T. rexes* lost teeth, their facial bones became distorted and knotted, and they grew a horn. In some ways, humans have turned out a lot like *T. rexes*—we lose our teeth as we grow and our facial bones change. If only we grew a horn, too . . .

SEE JANE'S BONES

In 2001, the skeleton of "Jane," an approximately eleven-year-old *T. rex*, was found in Montana. Jane's arms were found to be larger compared to her body than an adult *Tyrannosaurus*'s, and her shoulder joint seemed to be more moveable. This suggests that younger *T. rexes* were able to move more easily than the grown-ups. Jane's feet and legs were also found to be proportionally longer, which probably means that young *T. rexes* were faster runners than the adults.

Jane had seventeen curved and finely serrated teeth meant for ripping and tearing flesh, whereas an adult *T. rex* only had about

ten to twelve thicker teeth meant for grinding. Still, the jaw was perfectly suited to biting through prey, which at least suggests that juvenile *T. rexes* ate the same food as their parents. Does that mean Mom and Dad did the hunting and brought food back to the nest? No one can know for sure, but it is certainly a possibility.

GROWING PAINS

Humans and *T. rexes* are actually strangely similar. No, it's not that both have bone-crushing teeth, enormous size, or the ability to lay eggs. But the time it took for *T. rexes* to mature from juveniles to adults is comparable to the time it takes for humans to develop.

All dinosaur babies were extremely small. Most dinosaurs hit a growth spurt at ten years old (sometimes before), when their bodies changed shape and rapidly expanded to full adult size. *T. rexes*, on the other hand, began their growth spurts when they were about twelve years old, and the growing phase continued until they reached the age of eighteen or nineteen. Just like humans, the teenage years were an important developmental phase when lots of things—from appearance, to personality, to responsibility—changed for *T. rex*.

Scientists don't know for sure why the *T. rexes* had such a long childhood compared to other dinosaurs. One theory has to do with the other predators and prey that lived alongside *T. rex*. It turns out that *Tyrannosaurus rex* was fifty times (or more!) larg-

Juvenile *T. rexes* were able to move more easily than adults.

er than the next biggest predator in the area. This meant that adult *T. rexes* had easy access to large prey like duck-billed dinosaurs and sauropods. There were no mid-sized predators in this world, which means the mid-sized prey like troodontids and ornithomimosaurs should have gone uneaten—but they didn't. Instead, juvenile *T. rexes* had almost a decade to prey on these mid-sized dinosaurs without having to worry about competing with larger *T. rexes* for food.

Juvenile *T. rexes* preyed on mid-sized dinosaurs until they grew to their full size.

The Future of Studying the Past

PAUL SERENO IS ONE of the world's foremost experts on dinosaurs. In 2000 he said, "When I began [studying dinosaurs in about 1980], we knew almost nothing. It was just piles of bones everywhere. But now dinosaur paleontology has advanced on all fronts."

New technologies have allowed scientists to learn things about dinosaurs that would have been impossible just ten or twenty years ago. For example, CAT scanning the skulls of crested duck-bills like *Parasaurolophus* has helped scientists guess what kind of sounds the animals' air passages could have made. (They probably squeaked when they were young and bellowed in low frequencies as adults.)

Most scientists agree that the field of paleontology will advance in leaps and bounds in the coming years. So it is probable that we will learn a great deal more about dinosaurs, their babies, and their lives. In the meantime, the hunt for new information continues . . .

A Word About Wording

The study of dinosaurs is an exciting scientific discipline—and that's probably why it is filled with difficult, confusing, scientific words. Saurischians, Ornithischians, theropods, sauropodomorphs . . . it might feel like you'd need a brain the size of a *Giganotosaurus*'s mouth to keep it all straight. So here's a bit of a cheat sheet to help you out:

Biped: an animal that walks on two feet

Carnivore: an animal that eats meat

Embryo: a dinosaur baby forming in an egg

Excavate: to dig up bones

Herbivore: an animal that eats plants

Ornithischians: "bird-hipped" dinosaurs

Paleontologist: a scientist who studies fossils

Predator: the hunter

Prey: the hunted

Quadruped: an animal that walks on four feet

Saurischians: "lizard-hipped" dinosaurs

Sauropods: gigantic advanced sauropodomorphs that walked on four feet

Sauropodomorphs: plant-eating saurischian dinosaurs with long necks and small heads

Theropods: meat-eating saurischian dinosaurs that walked on two three-toed feet

Pronunciation Guide

Dinosaur terms can be hard to pronounce. Here's some help.

Albertosaurus: al-BERT-oh-SORE-us

Allosaurus: al-oh-SORE-us

Ankylosaurus: an-kill-oh-SORE-us

Apatosaurus: a-PAT-oh-SORE-us

Argentinosaurus: ar-gen-teen-oh-SORE-us

Brachyceratops: brak-ee-SERRA-tops

Camptosaurus: Camp-toe-SORE-us

Ceratopsid: SERRA-top-sid

Diceratus: die-SERRA-tus

Didelphodon: DIE-del-foh-don

Dimetrodon: DIE-meh-truh-don

Diplodocus: dih-PLAH-de-kiss

Eoraptor: EE-oh-rap-tor

Hadrosaurine: HAD-roh-SORE-een

Hadrosaurus: HAD-roh-SORE-us

Hypacrosaurus: high-PAK-roh-SORE-us

Hypsilophodon: hip-sih-LOH-foh-don

Iguanodon: ig-WAH-no-don

Lambeosaurine: LAMB-ee-oh-SORE-een

Maiasaura: my-ah-SORE-ah

Majungasaurus: mah-JUNG-ah-SORE-us

Mapusaurus Roseaea: MAP-ah-SORE-us rose-AY

Massospondylus: mass-oh-SPON-die-lus

Megaloolithus: meg-a-LOO-li-thus

Monoclonius: mono-CLOH-nee-us

Mussaurus: mus-OR-us

Ornithischia: or-ni-THISS-kee-ah

Orodromeus makelai: or-oh-DRO-me-us MA-keh-lie

Oviraptor philoceratops: OH-vih-rap-tor fie-loh-SERRA-tops

Pachyrhinosaurus: pack-ee-rye-no-SORE-us

Parasaurolophus: par-a-SORE-a-LOAF-us

Pentaceratops: penta-SERRA-tops

Plesiosaur: PLEE-see-oh-sore

Prosaurolophus: pro-SORE-a-LOAF-us

Protoceratops: pro-toe-SERRA-tops

Psittacosaurus: sih-tack-oh-SORE-us

Pterosaur: TARE-oh-sore

Saurischia: saw-RIS-kee-ah

Stegosaurus: STEG-oh-SORE-us

Styracosaurus: sty-RACK-oh-SORE-us

Therizinosaurus: THER-ih-ZINE-oh-SORE-us

Triceratops: try-SERRA-tops

Troodon: TROH-oh-don

Tyrannosaurus rex: tie-RAN-oh-SORE-us
   REX

Velociraptor: veh-LA-sih-rap-tor

Index